TOOLKIT #3

BECOMING A TECH-FOCUSED NONPROFIT

A guide for any small or medium-sized nonprofit to leverage the benefits of technology

WRITTEN BY:
MARILYN L. DONNELLAN, M.S.
MARGAUX S. PAGÁN

Becoming a Tech-Focused Nonprofit

One of the Nonprofit **Toolkit** series

Nonprofit Toolkits
Tool #1: Volunteer Handbooks
Tool #2: Sustainability Strategies
Tool #3: Becoming a Tech-Focused Nonprofit

Published by CreateSpace

©2018, by Marilyn L. Donnellan
Authors
Marilyn L. Donnellan, MS and Margaux S. Pagan

ISBN - 13: 978-1985374591
ISBN – 10: 1985374595

Table of Contents

Introduction

Nonprofits lose too much time and money with a hodgepodge of inadequate, outdated and inefficient technology and software. What a waste of donor funds! Or, on the opposite side of the equation, the confused, non-techie will respond to the flashy bells and whistles of the latest and greatest software sales pitch, spending too much money on something that doesn't integrate with what the nonprofit already has. To add to the frustration, especially in small nonprofits, many times there is no one on staff qualified or trained to use the software to its fullest capabilities.

We need to step back, take some deep breaths and re-think our entire process of technology and software development. In this guide we will provide techies and non-techies with step-by-step directions on how to establish workable solutions for identifying, integrating and developing every facet of the critical technology component of your organization. Although we have our favorite platforms, we intend to provide you with generic tools you can use to select what is best for your organization, rather than to try and tell you what you need or what we like.

The authors come from two totally different perspectives: one is a techie and one is a non-techie with three decades of nonprofit management experience. Whether you are a techie or non-techie, you will benefit from the field-tested suggestions because we've attempted to keep the "tech-speak" out of the equation.

However, a glossary is also included, just in case we slip up and a use a term you aren't familiar with. Included in the guide are:

- Rationales for technology and software needs assessments and inventories,
- Importance of the proper mind-set when dealing with technology,
- Strategies for developing technology vision and mission statements compatible with the organization's vision and mission,
- Steps for putting together a strategic, long-range technology plan,
- Suggestions for evaluating the nonprofit's software and web platform needs,
- Ways to understand the major components and silos in nonprofit technology and pitfalls,
- Steps for identifying programs that should integrate and/or be Cloud based and which address security concerns,
- Strategies for meshing software and technology needs,
- Budget development steps for short and long-term technology needs,
- Ways to get staff and board buy-in to technology improvements and planning by using a cost-benefit analysis, including investment in staff training,

- Roadblocks to technology development, such as platform silos, implementation difficulties, funding, documentation, technology advancements, etc.
- Examples of what works and what doesn't,
- Lists of possible resources and glossary of terms.

Chapter One

Technology: Help or Headache

The nonprofit had been serving the community for over 40 years, but they were struggling to keep their head above water. Donations were down and had been for the past three years. It didn't help they had seen three executive directors (ED) come and go in the same time frame either. The day the new ED walked in the door he discovered some big problems, many of which seemed to be directly tied to technology:

- The accounting was still being done using a simple bookkeeping software more suitable for an organization half their size;
- The donor database hadn't been updated in years and it wasn't integrated with the accounting software so there was no way to track who had been giving how much;
- There was no CRM (Customer Relationship Management) software or other donor or volunteer management software;
- The computers were all ten to fifteen years old and had inadequate memory;
- The only accounting back-up was a monthly back-up to flash drive which the bookkeeper took home with her, if she remembered;
- There was no one on staff with any type of technology expertise;

- The website hasn't been updated for two years.

To compound the problem, the finances were in such disarray the board was forced to hire a certified public accountant (CPA) to figure out the IRS 990 for the previous year, and that was going to cost more than $75,000. So, any hopes the ED had of upgrading the technology and software was probably not going to be approved by the board, at least not this year. And, it looked like the only way the ED could begin to build a donor database was to hire a staff person to start from scratch, an expenditure they really couldn't afford.

And that seemed to be just the tip of the iceberg. So where does the ED start to deal with the technology problems?

Unfortunately, this scenario or similar ones are not uncommon but are, in fact, repeated in too many nonprofits. Because this guide is focused on technology, I'm not even going to get into important issues like why wasn't the board keeping an eye on these things or why the frequent ED turnover? Important as those issues are, let's instead zero in on what appears to be some major roadblocks for ED's who find themselves in these types of situation:

- Inadequate funding,
- Outdated or inadequate website, technology and software,
- Lack of software interface or integration (the silo effect discussed in chapter three),
- Lack of knowledge or understanding of technology among staff,
- High staff turnover,

- A board who appears to have abdicated their responsibilities,
- Failure to keep donor database up to date.

Does this myriad of typical problems mean technology is really a help or just one big, never-ending headache for you and your nonprofit?

Each of the chapters in the guide will address these issues, providing a roadmap for anyone facing similar situations. In today's high-tech society, nonprofits who fail to keep pace with the advances in technology will lose out. Not only will they lose funding opportunities, but when donors, clients, potential donors, staff and volunteers see how outdated the nonprofit is in their use of technology, they will move on to serve within a more sophisticated, technologically savvy organization.

Just for grins, let's compare our problem nonprofit with one where upgrades in technology and software are a board-approved budget priority. This nonprofit is now about the same size budget wise as our problem nonprofit (about $2 million), but they have been growing steadily, doubling in size in the past five years. This is what they have in the way of technology:

- A website updated at least monthly and which includes all types of hyperlinks that make it easy for donors and volunteers to give and serve;
- An accounting system integrated with the fundraising software so when someone contributes, it is immediately recorded in both the accounting side and the CRM. If the donor is also a volunteer, the software flags the information;
- The accounting system includes a monthly budget component with comparisons between

actual, budget and previous year with percentage increase/decrease, as well as balance sheets;

- The accounting system allows for individual tracking of all grants and restricted funds, as well as gifts in kind;

- Copies of all legal documents (501c3 designation, 990s, W-2, bylaws, etc.) are filed on the Cloud;

- The CRM software includes volunteer development program records (recruitment, training, recognition and dismissal) for all types of volunteers (board, program, events, committee);

- The CRM software includes donor retention, recognition, planned-giving, leadership giving and follow-up, as well as pledges receivable and pledge loss;

- Programs use an outcomes measurements research and statistical software which interfaces with marketing strategies;

- Event software interfaces with the CRM software so records of volunteer involvement are kept up to date;

- Donor databases are updated at least weekly and are integrated with every method of giving: planned-giving, workplace giving, events, personal gifts, website, etc.;

- All software is backed up to the Cloud daily;

- Staff are trained when they are hired and re-trained at least annually on report features, software updates and technology upgrades;

- The board has approved a long-range strategic plan which includes adequate, budgeted funding for technology and software maintenance, security, upgrades and staff training,

• Project management software is used daily by all staff and incorporates the strategic planning goals monitored by the board;

• Equipment inventories and vendor records are computerized;

• All client, personnel, volunteer and donor records are computerized, password protected, with cyber security policies in place;

• All permanent records (including financial) are stored on the Cloud;

• A policies and procedures manual for all aspects of the nonprofit is available on the computer to all staff and board members, includes hyperlinks and is stored on the Cloud;

• All technology and software are updated and maintained regularly;

• A comprehensive, hyperlinked volunteer handbook is available on the website and includes volunteer applications, policies and procedures for recruitment, training, recognition and dismissal of all types of volunteers: board members, committees, program volunteers, virtual volunteers and volunteers with disabilities.

What a contrast between the two organizations! But how does a nonprofit move from scenario #1 to scenario #2? Does the ED have to be a techie (technologically savvy) person, or is it necessary to have on staff someone who understands hardware, software and maintenance?

And how do you pay for it? How can you avoid buying the wrong software, software that really doesn't fit with everything else you have? Or, avoid buying hardware that within a year or two is inadequate or out of date?

Believe me, I know from personal experience what an eye-rolling experience technology can be. I've gone from using a Selectric typewriter in my first nonprofit to a sophisticated, integrated, Cloud-based system in my last nonprofit, all in a little over twenty years. And I'm not a techie. In fact, the first solution that comes into my mind when I have problems with my computer? Pick it up and toss it out the window!

It is very difficult for my eyes to not glaze over when someone walks into my office and starts touting the features of some hardware or software we MUST have. And that gets me to some important recommendations to all you non-techies. These basic do's and don'ts really have nothing to do with any type of specific technology:

1. Don't be afraid to ask for definitions of terms or explanations. Too often we have a subconscious feeling we have to at least give the appearance of knowing everything. Check our glossary of terms (Addendum D) if you aren't sure of the meaning of something. Add terms to the glossary as you come across others you need to remember or better understand;

2. Do your homework and comparison shop before buying anything. Just like you wouldn't buy a car without carefully looking at costs of similar cars at other dealers, neither should you buy the first hardware or software package presented to you;

3. Do put together a technology committee of experts from your community to help you, especially if you do not have a techie on staff. We've included a sample job description as Addendum A;

4. Do plan. Think five to ten years down the road. I'll get more into this in the next chapter;

5. Don't forget to consider budget and staffing issues for anything you purchase, and that includes not just the costs of purchase but for any data entry, upgrades, maintenance, replacement and cybersecurity.

Chapter Two

Technology Inventories and Strategic Planning

Here is where I get to spout off about one of my favorite pet peeves: lack of strategic planning. Too many nonprofits operate from crisis to crisis rather than a board-approved strategic plan which is updated annually and based on organization-wide assessments. And, because of the rapidly changing environment in which nonprofits operate today, the outdated concept of strategic long-range planning not only won't work but is too unwieldy and usually outdated by the time the plan is completed. And this is a critical strategy for technology development.

I've solved the problem for you. I developed a simplified strategic planning process more than fifteen year ago. I was frustrated at the lengthy typical strategic planning process, out of date by the time you were finished with it. You can find it in my book, *Nonprofit Management Simplified: Board and Volunteer Development.*

A companion training module is also available to show you how to implement the process. This award-winning process will certainly not meet the demands of most academic requirements for strategic planning.

However, it has been field-tested by hundreds of nonprofits and I can guarantee it will help you jump-start your planning process if you haven't been doing annual strategic planning.

- **Fig. 1: Core Elements**

Strategic Planning and Accelerating Technologies

Fig. 1, the Core Elements graphic, shows how technology and strategic planning are key factors in every aspect of a successful nonprofit organization and must permeate and be integrated into all the six core elements: administration, programs, community involvement, marketing, resource development and board/volunteer development.

Too often both technology and strategic planning are relegated to the if-we-have-time-and-money-for-it strategy of management. For sustainable and successful nonprofits, that just won't work. Both MUST be regarded as critical for the achievement of the organization's vision and mission.

Be sure to include in the annual planning process inventories and assessments of your technology and software.

Addendum B includes examples of inventory and assessment forms. Re-write these forms to fit your needs. I recommend if, for example, you are doing your assessments and program evaluations in the six months prior to the beginning of your fiscal year, this is a great time to also do your technology inventory and assessment.

There are seven basic steps to building a technology plan.

Step #1: Inventory

It is helpful if every piece of your equipment and furniture already has inventory tags. You can find these at most office supply stores. Order them in consecutive numbers or use a label-maker and make your own. As you place the inventory tags on the items, record them either on a hand-held electronic device or on a written inventory sheet for transfer to a computerized form. Be sure to keep them in a secure location.

These types of inventories are essential for depreciation purposes. Your accountant will really appreciate your using this same format as Addendum B for every piece of capital equipment.

Be sure to check every department to inventory all furniture, electronic equipment and software. The technology inventory should include things like:

- Telephones (all communication devices, including land-lines, cellphones and any walkie-talkies or radios in automobiles owned by the nonprofit),
- Computers,
- Laptops and other hand-held devices,
- Printers,
- Security systems (including security cameras),
- Cameras, videos, projectors,
- Calculators and/or adding machines,
- Any specialized electronic equipment used with clients, such as medical devices,
- All software associated with every device in every department, including any online resources used, such as GoToMeeting, Eventbrite, Mailchimp, PayPal, Asana, the Cloud, etc. *Hint: Put inventory tags on the box the software came in or on the instruction manual.*
- Operating systems and processors (32-bit or 64-bit).

Step #2: Assessment

The technology assessment form (Addendum C) can be used to do a more in-depth analysis of your hardware and software in every department. It should evaluate how well the equipment works, looking for essential integrations across organizational silos (this will be dealt with more in chapter six).

As stated in the first chapter, too many nonprofits fail to make sure their software packages integrate across the various departments of the organization. Integration not only saves staff time by eliminating double entry of information but makes information more easily accessible by essential staff or volunteers.

For example: Susie Smith donated $1,000 to your nonprofit. Susie is also a volunteer, working as a child advocate. If your software is integrated across silos, her gift will be entered once when her check arrives in the accounting department, but the details will show up in the CRM software showing her as a donor. It will also indicate she is a volunteer who is donating, flagging her as someone eligible for recognition not only as a donor but also as a volunteer. The right CRM software will cut across what might be the silos of administration (accounting), resource development (fundraising), volunteer development (volunteer recognition), and programs (volunteer).

Without integrated software, the data on Susie's gift might have to be entered four different times by four different people into four different software packages instead of just once. Lack of integration can cost you more than if the money was spent up front for the right, integrated software. Not every software package will be able to integrate with every other package, but when it is possible, integration is extremely helpful and can, ultimately, be cost-saving.

As part of the assessment process, don't forget to survey all the folks who use your hardware and software. And that includes everyone: staff, volunteers, donors, website users, etc.

You might want to make the surveys anonymous, so you get the most candid responses. Ask them what they like, don't like; what works, doesn't work; what they need; what they wish they had; other platforms they recommend, etc. Summarize these results and include them in the goal-setting section of the strategic planning.

Annual inventories and assessments will be valuable tools for you in the strategic planning essential for growing your technology effectiveness.

Step #3: Set Direction

After completing the inventories and assessments, the critical next step in technology strategic planning is setting direction. One way to do this is to develop vision and mission statements for the technology side of your nonprofit. Hopefully, your nonprofit's vision and mission statements are current and reviewed at least every other year.

Establishing technology vision and mission statements is a simple way to establish clarity for where you want to go with technology in the future. Use the same techniques for vision and mission statement develop you would use for your nonprofit. This process is outlined in the Simplified Strategic Planning Training Module. The technology vision and mission statements could be developed by the technology committee and presented to the board during the annual strategic planning process.

For definition purposes, vision is "why" something is done, and mission is "how" the vision is accomplished. Vision statements have no action verbs, while mission statements are all about action. Examples of technology vision and mission statements are:

- Vision statement – All technology hardware and software enhancing the vision and mission of the organization;
- Mission statement – To implement hardware and software strategies which will support all facets of the nonprofit, build brand identity, operate efficiently across departments, be updated and maintained regularly and be secure from all potential breaches.

Step #4: Establish Measurable Goals

Challenge your board and staff to think futuristically when it comes to technology. Examples of your measurable goals might be:

- To centralize data within one year,
- To train all staff in use of new software within one year.

Look for software that will allow you to manage data across all the silos that currently separate your ability to get data. How quickly do you make program outcomes results available to donors and potential donors? What data are your donors, potential donors, volunteers, board members, staff and clients accessing?

How easy is the data to get to? Are your policies and procedures manuals computerized and hyperlinked for easy use? Can you track how they are accessing data? How long they stay on the various sections of your website?

Using the right software platforms is critical to not only better represent yourself via social media but it can also send clear messages to everyone connected to your organization that their time is valuable, and you are doing everything you can to make information easy to access.

Is your donor database interfaced with your accounting software? If it isn't, not only will double entry be required when someone donates, but mistakes are apt to be made in the data. How will you know if "thank-you" letters were sent when a contribution is made and the contact information for the donation is the same as what is in the donor database?

Fig. 2: Strategic Planning Process

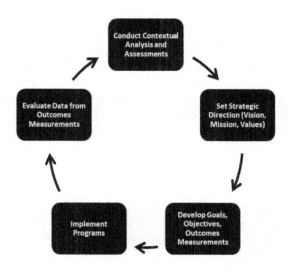

- **To purchase CRM software and enter all data within one year**

Customer Relationship Management (CRM) software or donor management software is essential for every nonprofit, not only to keep track of past and current donors but for recruiting potential donors. There are so many great software packages available you may find it difficult to choose the one perfect for your needs. But look for the one that will allow you to engage, re-engage and keep donors interest and giving.

Remember, every volunteer will usually be a good donor, so your CRM software should also double as a volunteer development database, or at least interface with it. I can't emphasize enough the importance of keeping this type of database up to date. I know of one non-profit executive director who was a fantastic fundraiser. He could pick up the telephone and easily get a million-dollar contribution when he needed it. But when he died suddenly, the nonprofit was in big trouble because he had never entered any of the donor information into a data base; it was all in his head. When he died, the donor data died with him.

- **To hire a marketing professional within two years**

One of the most important positions you need to fund nowadays at your nonprofit is for a well-paid, experienced and talented marketing professional. Without a good social boasting, branding and marketing strategy your nonprofit will get left in the fundraising dust. But for the best marketing in the world to work, you have to have technology and software that allows your program staff to be constantly updating the positive results of what you are doing within the community.

• **Within two years develop a unique fundraising strategy that will bring in at least $150,000 annually**
Today's donors respond to new and innovative approaches to fundraising, not the same-old, same-old. Just think about the millions of dollars raised with the ice-bucket challenge or which are raised every day through social media promotions of GoFundMe pages. Use your social media platforms to strategize for the newest exciting strategy to put your nonprofit on the fundraising map. And to do that you will have to have the technology and software to not only promote it but to respond to the donors and donations.

• **To develop a mobile platform for recording program outcomes**
There are a range of technologies to choose from to help program staff more quickly collect data about what they are doing in the field. Survey results, video messages from constituents, immediate results of quantitative program data with tools like Survey Monkey, can greatly speed up the time information gets from the field to the donor or prospective donor. Mobile devices can be used to track attendance and participation. Or maybe your strategic planning goals will include the need to develop a custom mobile application for recording program results. Gathering program

data will also require converting and analyzing it so you need special tools, such as computer assisted qualitative data analysis software. A computer search will help you find it. Just be sure you have the right technology to run the software and it is all included in the annual budget. If your nonprofit has not yet established an outcomes measurement-based system for all programs, you might want to look at suggestions on how to set it up in the book, *Nonprofit Management Simplified: Programs and Fundraising.*

Setting technology goals is where the strategic planning process itself is critical. These are just a few of the examples of goals you might set. If the leadership of the nonprofit (board and staff) work together in the annual planning process to develop a futuristic look at the technology and software needs of the nonprofit, they will be more apt to include money in the budget for it. Be sure to include goals for the purchase, updates and maintenance of hardware and software, as well as any training for staff. In some cases, you may also need to plan for hiring of staff for data entry, maintenance or consultants for cyber security (chapter six).

Step #5: Establish a Budget
Without a budget, there is no way you are ever going to be able to purchase the equipment and software you need. You may have to gradually add to your potpourri of equipment and software by prioritizing, based on what your budget will allow. But start somewhere with the most important components of what will eventually be a state of the art, integrated system. More about this in chapter five.

Step #6: Purchase, test, train and implement

As you begin to purchase the equipment, do your best to negotiate for trial periods to make sure it will work for you. If it doesn't work right, you need to have the right to return it within an agreed upon time for a full refund. It would be like buying a car without a warranty and finding out the transmission is faulty. You would never do that. Technology hardware and software has the potential to be very expensive, so make sure you do it right.

Then, of course, allow time to train staff and any volunteers who will be using the equipment and software. Never expect them to automatically know how to use it. Many companies include training in the price, so take advantage of the offer. Just be sure to accommodate the time needed for the training, allowing personnel time to learn it properly. And if, for some reason, an individual just cannot get used to the equipment or software, be prepared to either move them to another position or hire someone else. If knowledge of the new equipment will be a requirement for any position, be sure to add it to the job description.

Implementation strategies should have built into them some ways to evaluate how well they are working; which leads to the next strategy.

Step #7: Evaluate, update, maintain and re-evaluate

Most technology and software built today will be out of date tomorrow, so build into your planning the time and money for regular updates and maintenance. But first be sure you allow those using it the opportunity to tell you if it is doing what the manufacturer claimed it would do.

If it isn't working right, why update it? Or, if it is working well and an update is going to mess everything up, maybe the update should wait until the manufacturer corrects the bugs in the software or hardware.

Maintenance contracts are essential for all computers and software packages. Without regular updates on your software, you are more vulnerable to hacking. And, without good maintenance for your hardware, preventable breakdowns will cost you time and money.

And then, evaluate again and again. Accelerating technology strategies are all about constantly evaluating what you have with what you need, compared to what is available and what you can afford.

Chapter 3

Technology Interface and Silos

A huge issue for nonprofits are internal silos. Let me explain how this applies to technology and software. Too often data entry occurs in silos. Donor data, client data, staff data and volunteer data are entered into computers by different individuals via different software packages and different computers. Fig. 3 is an example of the typical silos in a nonprofit's database system.

Fig. 3 Technology Silos

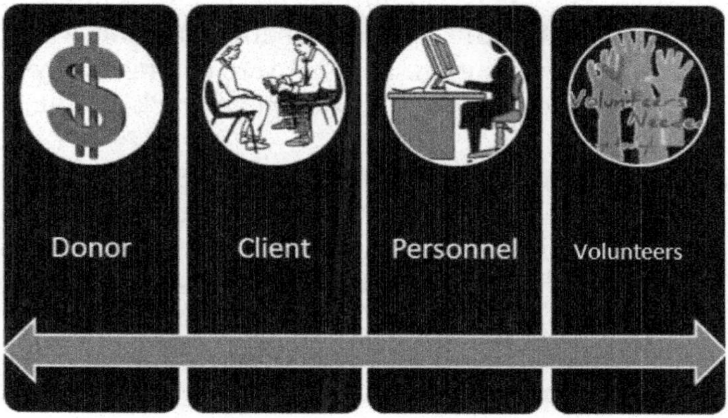

Donor   Client   Personnel   Volunteers

The result is often duplicate entries, greatly increasing the possibility of errors. These data entry silos also increase cyber security issues and the potential for fraud, simply because it is harder to keep track of multiple points of data entry. This can become a huge internal controls problem.

But there are solutions. Remember, many times donors are also volunteers, sometimes personnel and sometimes clients. Why would you need to enter the same data four different times? Wouldn't it save money and decrease errors if you had a CRM software package, which allowed all the data to interface, across all four silos? This software allows data to be entered once but be accessed at all four points or silos.

Let's say for example Susie Smith is a client. She decides to donate $25 during the annual fund drive. Her contact data is already entered into the CRM software as a client, so all the resource development staff has to do is now add her donation amount, so she can receive recognition. The software automatically is tied to the accounting department to track accounts receivable.

The same process applies, regardless of the data entry point. This not only solidifies internal controls and decreases costs, but greatly reduces fraud risks and errors. If the right software is chosen, it should also automatically generate thank-you notes from the correct department and record the gift into the appropriate recognition category.

What do I mean by "recognition category?" Great recognition programs include various levels of giving with corresponding recognition strategies. Leadership giving programs, for example, might have special lapel pins or other public recognitions for donors of $10,000 or more.

Your cross-silo software needs to include a way to track this type of giving so the right department or individual is notified so the correct recognition strategy is implemented.

This type of cross-silo planning takes work. But as I mentioned in chapter two, strategic planning related to technology requires implementation of the concept of accelerating technology:

Technology and software which is keeping pace with the strategic implementation of the vision and mission of the nonprofit across all six core elements and across all silos.

By making sure your software and hardware are interfaced, regularly updated, cyber secure and staff is adequately trained on how to use it, you are developing a dynamic and constantly evolving technology plan to help you achieve your mission. And, you are avoiding the trap of silos which can cost you money, time and put your organization at risk for errors and fraud.

Chapter Four

Choosing the Right Technology Solution

In our everyday lives, working with a nonprofit, we should not be shy to express ourselves on what is working and what is not working with our technology. Every single employee with the organization plays an invaluable role in supporting the mission. Whether you are part of the programs, resource development, senior leadership, or a volunteer, you are directly connected and engaged with everyday work it takes to support your clients and build life-impacting programs. This means your insight on everything from data entry to the selection of the right database is critical to your success.

We call this "staff buy-in." The powers that be are not the only ones who should make critical decisions in the selection of a database system, technology equipment, hardware, or how the technology will be used. Leaders of the organization can gain a wealth of knowledge by asking their most vital asset: the employees. Including them in the conversation early and often is critical to both short-term and long-term success.

Create an advisory committee to the technology committee, composed of employees from each department. The advisory committee's main purpose is to bring staff's unique thoughts and insight into the conversation to ensure practical implementation issues, which aren't obviously apparent, are highlighted, noted and considered. You might want to put together a job description for the advisory committee, like the technology committee's job description (Addendum A), just to make sure everyone is clear on their roles and responsibilities.

If you have a small staff (five or less), it might be helpful to expand the expertise by incorporating outside experts. Connect with the local technology community. There might be university or college students looking for service learning projects, or for-profit business professionals actively seeking service opportunities. Some companies have volunteer requirements for their staff. Take advantage of that requirement and incorporate their talent into your technology committee. Their expertise will not only expand your network but can help your nonprofit improve its knowledge of technology.

Recently, I had a conversation with a nonprofit executive director who really gets this concept of spreading your network widely. His methods of achieving success centered around the idea and practice of "partnerships in funny places." In other words, he looks for volunteers and knowledge input in unexpected locations. And it works.

As a nonprofit leader or professional, it is our duty to look beyond our comfort zone and spread into networks we may not have immediate or direct connections with. Opportunities are everywhere.

We must remain open-minded to where, when and how those connections occur, especially when building your technology solutions. Expanded contexts are vastly important, even more so for small nonprofits, in order to garner the support you need to build from within so your organization is professional, engaging and managed with appropriate stewardship. And folks you bring in as technology advisors, often become your biggest financial supporters.

Once you have recruited the necessary internal and external resources and information, as outlined in chapters one through three, it is time to combine forces with your staff, board members and internal volunteers. Rallying the troops on technology issues will take a kind of tender caress to ensure everyone is on-board and actively participating in the conversations. Some hints for increasing buy-in and positive communication include:

1. Establish a clear liaison or leader

Who will be the gatekeeper of all relevant information, be responsible for communication to and from all members of the committee? This individual should be selected by the staff and/or board involved with the process and planning for technology. It might be your IT (Information Technology) person, if you are fortunate enough to have one on staff. Regardless of who it is, the individual must maintain the selected structure and focus on the mission of the committee and its goals. A lot of confusion can be avoided if everyone knows who the leader or project manager is from the very beginning of the discussion.

2. Announce the project's intentions internally

Everyone (staff, volunteers, board members), even those not directly involved with the process, need to be made aware of the project and what is happening, since it might impact what they are doing. For example, technology inventories and surveys will impact everyone in the nonprofit who handles technology. This type of announcement can be done via email, staff meetings or at special meetings. Just be sure everyone is notified in advance.

3. Identify and express the roles and responsibilities of the committee

Give everyone a chance to meet the project leader. We all work better when there are clear pipelines of information. If you incorporate virtual volunteers in your nonprofit or volunteers with disabilities, be sure you include them via online conference communications, too.

4. Create and communicate expectations

We cannot generate positive responses if we have not properly communicated what is expected of everyone. Provide clear lists of incentives, goals, timelines, expectations, and implications on every aspect of the project.

5. Follow-through

Keep lines of communication open during and after the project(s). It is natural to grow weary or even confused the longer a project continues. Any team can lose sight of the overall goal. It is the committee's, and particularly the leader's, responsibility to communicate often with everyone on project goals' progress. Likewise, non-committee members, particularly the board, must hold the committee accountable for goal completion.

Working together, cohesively, is the glue which holds any organization together. All departments will naturally be swept away with daily requirements of their individual jobs. Integration is key to bringing all the moving parts, all the opinions, and all the priorities under one umbrella: the mission. Everything the nonprofit does should always follow the overall vision and mission. When the team comes together to consider if a grant is appropriate, or wants to know if approaching a potential sponsor is appropriate, for example, the up-front question is always: "How will this help us achieve our vision and mission?"

And the same thing applies to the technology committee. The answer to the question cannot and should not come from one person but should include the insight and direction of the entire committee.

Another way to look at this is to imagine a car's engine. If the cylinders begin to act independently of the pistons, the engine would not be able to ignite. The car would not be able to start. Each moving piece within a nonprofit is part of a larger engine working together to fulfill the intended mission. Integration of all these pieces or parts begins with the senior leaders. They essentially drive the organization's cultural engine. Integration is a cultural dynamic. Nonprofits who lack this dynamic or culture, will struggle to implement a technology plan.

Integration is essential for a good technology solution. Yet it will be unique for each organization and be implemented very differently.

The psychological definition of integration is, "the organization of the constituent elements of the personality into a coordinated, harmonious whole." And that's exactly what you want with your technology. If you have worked within a nonprofit harmoniously coordinated, you have seen the equivalent of a very rare nonprofit utopia. There are major differences between a technologically integrated nonprofit and a siloed nonprofit.

"Integration" in the tech world is a term used to explain the process of data flowing between systems. Increasingly, the term has crossed over into the non-tech realm to refer to gaps or silos within a workplace or community. Here, we will use both connotations – community sectors and technology – to understand and adopt an integrated culture of human assets to technology solutions. Fig. 3 in the last chapter showed how data silos impact an organization. Fig. 4 shows how integration benefits an organization.

The chart shows only a fraction of the total benefits involved with integrating the organization's culture to improve the outcomes because of technology decisions and adoption. Let's look at each of these benefits in greater detail.

1. **Data Integrity**
   So much within a nonprofit is dependent on the input and output of a technology solutions, such as a database or CMR system.

"Dirty data in. Dirty data out," is a common mantra among those involved in reporting processes. It means we must be able to trust the data we put into our financial system, programs, fundraising and outcomes measurements.

Fig. 4 – Benefits of Integration

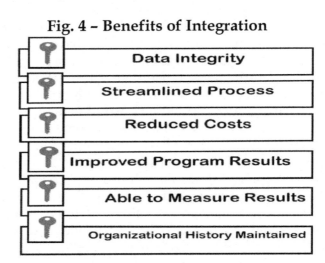

The tools we use give us the capacity to provide stakeholders and the public with information on our success. It is common in siloed organizations for data to be incomplete, inconsistent or incorrect, or "dirty." Integration with a CRM software helps to develop organizational practices which ensure data input into the system is correct. Staff is equipped, then, with the know-how to enter or sync relevant and valuable data related to every aspect of the nonprofit. This includes data on clients, programs, volunteers, employees and donors. This valuable data must be accurate, so staff and volunteers know, consistently, it is reliable.

2. Streamlined Processes

Between departments a lot of activity happens within the nonprofit. What may work for one department may not work for another. Different processes exist inter-departmentally and organization wide. For the sake or discussion, let's focus on the context of technology streamlining processes between departments for the benefit of the entire nonprofit.

Imagine one department maintains all their data and project management on a spreadsheet, while the rest of the organization uses a CRM or other project management system. Over time, this would cloud the validity of data output, not only because different systems were being used, but because the results would be different.

However, if the same project management software is used in every department, it would create a flow of data and information across all departments, like a train network or the way a river flows evenly and smoothly into the canals and lakes and streams.

3. Reduced Costs

Cost reduction is a pretty obvious benefit. Integration can have a major impact on reducing expenses, such as reducing paper, ink and duplication of work. Plus, as integration takes hold in an organization, so is communication improved.

When we have concise processes in place, we reduce the highest costs in any organization: soft costs, or the function costs. In other words, the more integration we have, the better and more efficiently we work, and the better and more efficiently we work, the less personnel expenses we have.

4. Improved Program Results

With the right data, your team can highlight the impact your programs are having on people, the environment, or animals your mission is helping. You can garner increased support from foundations, corporations or individuals. You can communicate with your constituents in a strategic manner with the program results they care most about. You can learn from the data you are capturing and create new or expand existing programs. Integrated data is your best friend to improve program results.

5. Able to Measure Impact

In recent years, more funders have taken up the case against preventing starvation cycles in nonprofits. For years, nonprofits were restricted on how much they could spend on overhead costs, leading to increasing hardship and a sense of "starvation" at not being able to accomplish their mission due to lack of adequate administrative resources. But, without staff, lights and adequate operations expenses, we cannot run programs effectively.

The trend away from forcing starvation cycles within the sector is leading to more discussion around measuring impact and measuring return on investment (ROI) in order to calculate success or effectiveness. And without the right outcomes measurements from our programs, and without the correct allocation of costs into administrative, program and fundraising categories, it is impossible to effectively convey impact and ROI to funders.

6. Organizational History Maintained

Integration promotes a cohesive historical structure, leading to long-term sustainability. Why is this important? First, data collection of historical data which analyzes fundraising costs and success is essential in order to plan future funding strategies. Long-term financial stability is foundational to long-term sustainability for any nonprofit.

Secondly, nonprofits have high rates of staff turnover, which can lead to a loss of institutional memory. Solid technological systems which archive policies and procedures ensure long-term sustainability by keeping the information readily accessible, regardless of staff and volunteer turnover. And, finally, funders often want historical financial data which only a good database can provide.

Take another look at the job description for the technology committee in Addendum A. Notice that resource and needs assessments which evaluate technology systems is a big part of the committee's responsibility. How can the committee do this type of evaluation? There are seven steps to an effective technology assessment, spearheaded by the committee.

Step #1: Organize the committee

One of the things to do, is provide each member of the committee with an overview of the committee's responsibilities (Addendum A).

The chair of the committee, at the first meeting, should facilitate a discussion of the goals and objectives. One of the goals might be to develop the assessment tool; something similar to Addendum C. Some of the questions the assessment might need to answer include:

- What is the expected result of this committee's work? (vision and mission)
- What type of technology solutions should we seek to adopt?
- How will adopting this technology solution meet our nonprofit's strategic goals and needs?
- Who will this technology solution directly impact?
- Who needs to give us input?
- What is our target annual budget for the technology? Maintenance, upgrades, cybersecurity, training, purchase, etc.?
- What is our timeline?

Step #2: Assign roles

Each committee member should be assigned a specific role or task. Besides the committee chair and vice chair, other committee positions might include:

- Research leader: Gathers and coordinates all research collected by committee (chapter two)
- Secretary: Takes meeting minutes; coordinates and schedules meetings; serves as liaison between the nonprofit and committee

- Finance leader: Ensures committee stays within budget; interprets all financial implications to the nonprofit
- Technology leader: Should be someone with a technology background; knows how to ask the tough questions and align the organization's overall technology structure with the functionality of the proposed technology solutions.

Step #3: Conduct the assessment

Using a form like Addendum C, everyone who uses technology in the organization is asked to evaluate its effectiveness: what works, what doesn't work, how it could be improved, what is missing, etc. This might include clients, volunteers and staff. The assessment is then put into a summarized report by the research lead/chair.

Step #4: Create a checklist

The technology lead/chair develops a checklist, based on the assessment and on their knowledge of what other platforms are available. The checklist might list items by categories, such as: "must have," "not as important," "be nice to have, but not essential."

By using a prioritized checklist for developing technology solutions, the committee will be better able to develop a technology plan. Some ways to collect this information from employees, volunteers, and clients might include:

- Send an email to everyone with a pre-formatted spreadsheet listing all or most features of a typical technology solution. For example: email integration with Constant Contact;

volunteer management software; volunteer applications posted on the website, etc. The spreadsheet file could be placed on a shared drive or Drobox.

• Have meetings with the various groups where the project is shared, and the spreadsheet is handed out. Explain how to fill in the spreadsheet and due dates.

• Meet individually with department heads or key staff or volunteers for their input.

Step #5: Develop a plan
Based on the results of the assessment and checklist, the technology committee develops a prioritized, short and long-term technology plan and budgets.

Step #6: Schedule demo meetings with vendors of the top two to three solutions
Before finalizing the plan, set demo meetings with the vendors for the top two to three technology solutions proposed by the committee. Have them walk through the software or open-source solutions while the committee asks questions. Once the demos are complete, finalize cost estimates and budgets (chapter five).

Step #7: Present technology plan to the senior staff and board leadership
Using a variety of presentation tools, including visuals, the technology committee chair presents an overview of the work done by the committee and their recommendations. Generally, this would include a three to five-year plan for purchase, upgrades, training, cybersecurity, budget and recommendations

on the types of hardware and software needed and why.

Don't forget to include in the presentation the expected long-term benefits of the plan, as well as how the plan will be updated annually.

Once the plan is approved, the fun begins: implementation. The big challenge will be making sure you are integrating your technology solutions across every platform: website, database, email service provider (mass and internal), online donation solution provider, accounting software, program software, project management tools, hardware, volunteer management software, program management software, operating systems, etc.

This phase will require you to live in both the short-term and long-term worlds. That's because you must consider what you want and need in the next three months to a year, while simultaneously creating a vision of where you want to be in three to five years.

Chapter Five

Developing a Technology Budget

Once we have a better sense of what our technology needs and wants are, we can begin conducting research to find solutions and develop the budget for technology. One of the best ways to do this is to conduct a cost-benefit analysis. A huge advantage to this method is how effective it can be in convincing the board of the validity of the technology needs. Using this method, you are not only comparing precise costs to options, but you are also comparing the benefits with the solutions from a cost perspective.

For example, when choosing between CRM version A and CRM version B, a cost-benefit analysis will help you evaluate the hard costs for purchasing the CRM, maintenance and training, PLUS analyze the plug-ins and add-ons available as built-in features. What this does is show the senior staff leadership and key volunteers the long-term cost benefit.

A more complex way to use a cost-benefit analysis is to compare soft-cost savings, such as "implementing a new CRM saved $5,000 by reducing paper and printing costs and staff time."

Or, "We purchased the donor tracking software and our return on investment (ROI) for just one month was $50,000, because we were able to identify 50 new donors."

Or, "Because we invested in the research and statistical software, our return on impact (ROI) was $100,000, because we were able to demonstrate the effectiveness of our program outcomes to XYZ Foundation, which gave us a grant for $100,000."

When you use this method of comparison in developing a budget, it allows for an appropriate assessment and builds trust in the technology selection process. To help you with these types of assessments, there are many free or low-cost templates available online. Go to Addendum F for a list of some helpful templates.

It is the finance leader's responsibilities to fill in the appropriate costs for each technology item listed in the budget. This may sound like a simple task. However, it can become complicated as you begin to project technology needs three or five years down the road. It is recommended to think over-budget, rather than work conservatively, even adding a five percent cushion for unexpected costs. In addition to the technology needs listed in the budget, don't forget upgrades, replacements, programming, security, and any possible customizations in the long-term budget planning. For example:

- Will the organization's website need to be revamped in the next five years?
- If we grow as we expect, will our current technology support the growth?

Appendix E is an example of a budget format to consider.

Chapter Six

Avoiding Common Pitfalls

There are major pitfalls nonprofits need to avoid when working on technology issues: silos, funding, overhead cost limitations, cybersecurity, updates, etc. While there are more, this chapter will focus on these specific issues which can hinder your ability to implement your technology plan.

Although we talked about silos in chapter three, it is so critical when dealing with technology issues, I am reminding you again of its importance. The term "silos" has become infamous for disconnected or disorganized. Many nonprofits are investing time and resources to close the gap between their departments to be more transparent and be more unified to the outside world. Working without silos is a major challenge; but one with a simple solution:

Keep your organization's mission at the forefront of your work and silos cannot exist.

When your mission is the driver in everything you do, departments, personnel and even funders cannot set your organization's agenda. Leadership inside and outside the nonprofit is responsible for ensuring silos are dissolved.

Technology has a unique role as a unifier for the entire organization. Every staff person using a computer has a server with a network-protected file system, sending confidential emails essential for the mission. This dynamic produces a silo-free perspective. Where the challenge occurs is when technology needs are decided within a department, rather than with input of the entire organization.

For instance, the development department has a strategy to utilize a mass email provider, such as Constant Contact or MailChimp, to improve engagement and management with volunteers. This strategy is owned by the development team. However, the volunteers are supporting programs, too. In a silo-free work environment, the program and development teams will work together on this strategy, with both teams involved in the decision of email provider and the content of the email.

To reach this pinnacle of technology adoption, the right funding is necessary. We are all too familiar with the "not applicable for operational expenses" line item in grant applications and fund request guidelines. As you will see in Appendix E, there are many costs involved in the journey to technology nirvana. You will need funding for hardware, software, security, equipment licenses, and, most importantly, to compensate staff.

At the most basic level, you will need the following technology systems:

- Telephone,
- Internet,
- Computer hardware,

- Computer software (i.e. Microsoft Office, which includes Word, Excel, Power Point, etc.; project management software),
- Donor databases (CRM, recognition),
- Website,
- Email (i.e. Access, MailChimp, Mad Mimi)
- Accounting,
- Cloud storage (i.e. iCloud, Dropbox, OneDrive, Google Drive, etc.).

Beginning with these systems, think about what kind of funding you need to function at the most efficient level. Identifying your organization's core funding needs is the first step in determining who and what you will ask of your supporters and funders.

Let's imagine all the above basic systems total $25,000 per year. The figure includes everything: hardware, software, security, licenses and staff. Now, you need to ask some questions:

- How many of these are onetime costs and how many will be on-going costs to be built into the annual budget?
- Who should we ask for the one-time costs? What other resources (such as in-kind) will we explore?
- Can we cover the costs with existing funds (such as a capital fund)? If so, how much? What still needs to be paid for?
- Do we need additional funds to cover incidentals, such as equipment malfunctions, security breaches, etc.? If so, what should that contingency amount be?
- Who will we contract with to maintain our hardware and software systems?

- How will be allocate these costs across administration, fundraising and programs?

There are a variety of resources available to help fund your technology needs. For example:

- Ask individual board members,
- Cultivate a long-time individual donor; maybe one with an interest in technology,
- Charge the technology committee to create a "giving circle" or "major donor" technology campaign,
- Connect with TechSoup for equipment and software grants,
- Connect with your local tech community to recruit volunteer or pro-bono services: NetSquared, Tech4Good, local universities and colleges, city tech initiatives, etc.,
- Subscribe to The Foundation Center to look for technology-focused grant opportunities,
- Google Grants provides nonprofit organizations up to $10,000 in AdWords funding to increase online advertising, including search engine optimization and marketing efforts,
- Companies like Cisco, IBM, Verizon, Dell and AT&T provide a wide variety of grant funding opportunities for nonprofits.

Many conversations across the nonprofit sector concern the overhead costs issue. More and more funders, both private and public, are beginning to realize the importance of allocating a specific portion of a grant fund to cover technology and other overhead expenses.

As we discussed before, funders are realizing the restrictions on overhead costs to ten percent or less was creating starvation hardship cycles for nonprofits, making them unable to sustain their efforts. That's why the conversation between funders and nonprofits has changed to a more honest, realistic look at what it costs to provide quality programs and achieve long-term solutions to community problems. And, technology is a major factor in achieving any nonprofit's mission.

How do you have this kind of conversation with your existing funders and donors? If you have a strong relationship with them, sit down with them and discuss allocating a percentage of their funding to support your technology plan. Start with making the case by using the cost-benefit analysis we talked about in chapter five. Show how growth, efficiency and effectiveness of programs are directly aligned with technology.

Making the case for technology funding will involve taking a close look at the impact your technology will have on every function of your nonprofit. For instance, by adopting a CRM system, can you demonstrate how it will help to engage and recruit more volunteers? By upgrading and revamping your website, will you have more visibility, brand identity and marketing power, thus raising more funds?

Create a one-page document to illustrate the impact and/or improvements achieved because of the adoption or implementation of specific hardware or software. In other words, outcomes measurements aren't just for programs. When you can demonstrate positive outcomes because of improved and upgraded technology, you will be able to get more funding.

Training hasn't been mentioned yet. But it is very important. Opportunities for continuing education and growth must be ongoing. Training can come in many forms: on-site staff training, one-on-one coaching, online classes, YouTube videos, webinars, workshops and seminars, etc.

There will never be a shortage of chances to expand your knowledge on how to better use a tool, platform, or how to incorporate a new practice. Your learning gaps and budget will determine the type of training needed. Also, changing factors, such as staff turnover rates will impact your training plans.

Remember, if your team is not adequately skilled at supporting the technology in which you have invested time, money and resources, there will be a deficit in dollars or benefit.

Another common pitfall for many organizations is security, believing they cannot afford risk management insurance or essential cybersecurity systems. But, with so many cloud-based systems available today, much of the security responsibility has shifted to the provider (Google, Salesforce, Microsoft, etc.) to secure your data. These providers invest billions to secure their customers' information. However, even they have glitches in their systems. Hackers all over the world jeopardize sensitive personal data of your donors, employees, volunteers and clients (social security numbers, credit card numbers, birth dates, etc.). The media frequently headlines breaches of data in companies like Target, Equifax and Home Depot. Each of these companies was forced to spend billions to rectify the impact of the breaches.

Imagine the financial and public relations impact on your nonprofit if your data is breached. The loss of your loyal donor, employee, volunteer and client sensitive data could have long-term effect on the integrity of your organization.

I cannot emphasize enough the importance of you taking responsibility for the security of every piece of data in your organization. Network and data security provider programs can be expensive. Since budget is usually a major issue in most nonprofits, look for a local resource or independent consultant to help you identify cybersecurity resources. Contact your local technology school or community college. Look for pro-bono providers or offer to trade value with a small business for the service. Some risk management resources are listed in Addendum F.

One big caution, however. Don't assume your young cousin or nephew, who might be a gung-ho techie, is knowledgeable enough to implement the right cybersecurity system. You need a professional for a job like this.

There are three specific security issues you need to be sure your technology updates and cybersecurity include: PCI (Payment Card Industry) compliance, software updates, and general risk management.

PCI compliance involves the protection of data transferred between merchants, software developers and merchants or service providers, usually via credit cards. Often credit cards are the primary source of transactions for donations or event ticket sales in nonprofits. PCI security standards require every business accepting credit cards comply, including nonprofits. The standards are available at **https://www.pcisecuritystandards.org/**.

Next on our list of security are those pesky and annoying alerts notifying us of new software update. What you may not realize is how important these are to prevent security breaches. Outdated software is an invitation for hackers to access your data and systems. This applies to any software your organization is using, including:

- Operating systems,
- File management systems,
- Applications,
- Computer drivers,
- Databases,
- Websites.

Do not ignore these updates! If you are unsure about doing the updates, developers will typically include a complete description of the updates to help you assess the implications to your organization.

Finally, your entire nonprofit must include risk management planning as a standard operating procedure. By establishing an overall risk management plan for every department and system, it will give the volunteer and staff leadership a better understand of how to respond in case of a risk emergency. The book, *Nonprofit Management Simplified: Internal Operations,* includes some step by step directions for setting up an organizational risk management plan.

The basics of a risk management plan related to technology will include the following:

- Detailed system configuration documentation (related to the technology inventory discussed in chapter two),
- Identification of threats and vulnerability (this could be added to the inventory assessment)

- Risk mitigation (part of the risk management assessment and plan),
- Assessments and implementation,
- Security practices and frequent testing.

When someone says the word, "security," don't panic. Different organizations and individuals have various understandings of technology security. Remember, every time we visit a website or use login credentials, we are putting ourselves, our networks and our nonprofit at risk. This is precisely why companies like Google, Amazon and Salesforce spend millions (if not billions) of dollars every year ensuring our information is secure. And, there are ways your small or medium-sized nonprofit can find solutions to security issues when you make security issues a priority, ensuring you can achieve your mission with confidence and data dignity.

Let's use an example of a mid-sized nonprofit with a budget of $3 million. They decided to move their database from a software-based solution to a cloud-based system: Salesforce. During the planning discussions, the topic of security came up. Salesforce is a multi-billion-dollar enterprise offering CRM solutions to for-profits and nonprofits. Our hypothetical nonprofit knew Salesforce offered 10 free licenses per year to receive their security solution. So, they applied and received one of the free licenses, thus procuring an expensive cybersecurity solution for free. Salesforce assured them they work hard to protect sensitive data of all customers, so the nonprofit could focus on securing their internal network; a win-win.

Many nonprofits build their websites on CMS (Content Management Systems), such as WordPress or Wix). These systems have their own built-in security measures. However, with the help of a web specialist or an IT security administrator, you can add your own security checkpoints and processes for your website. This is where your multiple outside contacts will come in handy. Leverage the talents of your board, committees (like the Technology Committee) and staff to stay within budget.

Always remember, however, the cheapest might not be the best. If you have some wiggle room in the budget, find an outside source willing to offer cybersecurity services with a barter for sponsorship of a major event or at a discounted rate. They receive great marketing opportunities and you get professional cybersecurity for your website.

The world of technology does not have to be filled with landmines. Taking it step by step will help ease the angst and hesitations. Carefully evaluate the risk management issues through regular assessment. Establish cybersecurity plans which are regularly tested and upgraded.

Everything we do as nonprofits has risks associated with it. It part of what we do. However, navigating these risks on the technology side and seeing the pitfalls before you fall into them will help you stay on track and achieve your mission.

Chapter Seven

Keeping Technology at the Forefront

We all have the best intentions when setting out on any new venture. Creating a technology-centric organization is no different. The work continues even after you have implemented the right systems, the policies and procedures are in place, everyone is trained, and everything is secure.

Now comes maintenance, evaluation and adjustment of your technology plan. Maintenance is a never-ending process which will last as long as your nonprofit does. But, long-term sustainability for the nonprofit, including your technology, does not happen without constant upgrading and maintenance. You want to ensure all technology systems run properly, including your website, network, databases/CRM, email, and even your external systems.

In your technology planning, you might want to perform maintenance checks weekly, monthly or quarterly. I recommend you develop a checklist form listing every system requiring maintenance and when. The frequency of maintenance is up to you and what works for your nonprofit.

At different stages, you will need to grow with technology advances. As mentioned before, this is known as an "accelerating technology." Along the way, you may want to add a new feature or tweak your systems to facilitate new programs, new initiatives or simply the growth of the organization.

Let's suppose, for example, you now see a need for a new donor recruitment strategy. Your strategic plan includes a goal to execute an email sign-up, with a pop-up on your website to capture new names to cultivate and convert into donors. This seems simple enough, right? But have you considered the following issues, essential for making this happen?

- Does your current web platform allow for form integration with your CRM? This helps reduce time spent on manual data entry and reduces data entry errors.
- Can your current web platform enable pop-up windows? Or will you need to bring in a web developer to write custom code?
- If you are offering a premium or value-added proposition to the potential donor, who on staff will be notified and how will you be able to fulfill it?
- Is your email service provider (i.e. MailChimp or Constant Contact) enabled to send automatic responses to start immediate engagement with the potential donor?

These are, of course, only a few questions to answer on an issue like this, which initially seems straight forward. There might be a lot of other questions you would need to ask.

Finally, individuals and organizations are in a constant state of change, whether we like it or not. With new technologies available to us every day, and new ways to communicate, it is easy to quickly feel overwhelmed with the possibilities. This is where planning comes in.

In our donor recruitment strategy example, what happens after the implementation plan has run its course? Do we take the pop-up window down? Better yet, what if our current web platform caused us to spend over our budget to hire an outside web developer? Do we investigate other platforms with greater flexibility to meet our needs now and into the future? Do we hire a web master on a monthly contract to do upgrades?

Our goal should be for our technology to keep up with our nonprofit's growth. Adjustments to our technology plan should be expected and welcomed. But that will not happen without engaging board, staff and donors in an enthusiastically supported and funded, accelerating technology approach.

Job Description

<u>**Title:**</u> Technology Task Force or Committee*

<u>**Responsible to:**</u> Board of Directors or Internal Operations or Administration Committee, * or the technology staff person

<u>**Purpose of Committee:**</u> The development of policies, budget development and monitoring of year-round technology hardware software needs and implementation

<u>**Key Responsibilities:**</u>

1. Planning—To develop short and long-range goals and advise the staff on action steps for goal completion,

2. Resource and Needs Assessments—To assess community, volunteer, staff and internal resources available and needed to support all facets of technology hardware, software, upgrades and staff training,

3. Policies and Procedures – To develop policies to present to the board on all technology issues and provide advice to the staff on the development of procedures for implementation of the policies,

4. Budget—To develop and monitor policies and procedures for the development of the annual technology budget, including the procurement, upgrade and maintenance of hardware, software, staff training, and staff needs,

5. Legal—To develop policies and monitor cyber security procedures related to donor, volunteer, client and staff confidential information,

6. Technology/Equipment—To evaluate and

recommend procurement of equipment suitable for the efficient and effective fulfillment of the objectives of the organization,

7. Board Communications—To keep the board of directors informed on the implemented strategies, results of administrative efforts and any potential policies needed, that will allow for efficient and effective internal management that meets total quality management standards.

Committee Structure:

The chairman of the committee shall be a member of the board of directors and shall select, or cause to be selected, a vice chairman. The chairman and vice-chair shall also serve as members of the executive committee and shall keep the board informed on the committee's oversight of board-approved, committee goals. A majority of the committee shall be board members. Sub-committees or short-term task force groups may be formed to complete the committee's objectives.

Time Commitment:

At least one meeting per month, or as needed to fulfill the committee's goals.

* In smaller communities, this could be a sub-committee of the administration or internal operations committee.

Addendum B
Sample Technology and Software Inventory Form
Include all hardware, software and digital equipment

Date of inventory: _____
Person doing inventory:
_____

Item	Description	Date of Purchase	Cost	Date removed from inventory

Addendum C
Sample Technology Assessment

Date of assessment: _____

Person doing assessment:

_____

Item	Description	Integrates with	Problems or Need

Addendum D
Glossary of Terms

Accelerating Technologies – *Technology and software which is keeping pace with the strategic implementation of the vision and mission of the nonprofit across all six core elements and across all silos.*

Applications - An application program (app or application for short) is a computer program designed to perform a group of coordinated functions, tasks, or activities for the benefit of the user.

Bit - A bit (short for binary digit) is the smallest unit of data in a computer. A bit has a single binary value, either 0 or 1. Although computers usually provide instructions that can test and manipulate bits, they generally are designed to store data and execute instructions in bit multiples called bytes.

Byte - Abbreviation for binary term, a unit of storage capable of holding a single character. On almost all modern computers, a byte is equal to 8 bits. Large amounts of memory are indicated in terms of kilobytes (1,024 bytes), megabytes (1,048,576 bytes), and gigabytes (1,073,741,824 bytes).

CMS – Content Management Systems are software applications or a set of related programs that are used to create and manage digital content. CMSs are typically used for enterprise content management (ECM) and web content management (WCM).

CPU – Central Processing Unit is the computer's brain; where information is processed.

CRM – Customer Relations Management Software – Software which allows the nonprofit to integrate all facets of data: accounting, donations, recognition and volunteer development.

Gigabytes – See "Byte"

Hard Drive - Where most of the information on the computer is stored

IT – Information Technology

Megabytes – See "Byte"

Networking – How the computer connects to the internet or other networked devices

Operating System - An operating system (OS) is the program that, after being initially loaded into the computer by a boot program, manages all the other programs in a computer. The other programs are called applications or application programs.

Ports – Device ports are how the computer connects to other devices, let keyboard, mouse, printer, etc.

Processor - A central processing unit (**CPU**) is the electronic circuitry within a computer that carries out the instructions of a computer program by performing the basic arithmetic, logical, control and input/output (I/O) operations specified by the instructions. Most are either 32-Bit or 64-Bit. 64-Bit computers are faster.

RAM – Random Access Memory is where information is temporarily stored while the computer is running; not the same as storage, which allows you to keep information.

SEO - Search Engine Optimization is the practice of increasing the quantity and quality of traffic to your website through organic search engine results.

Addendum E
Sample Budget
All costs are estimates and based on a nonprofit with 10 staff.

Category (staff costs extra)	Quantity	Cost each	Est. Total
Hardware			
Telephones	10	$460	$4,600
Internet	1	$3,000	$3,000
Computers	10	$2,500	$25,000
Maintenance			
Maintenance (monthly fee)	12	$150	$1,800
Monthly updates (hardware/software)	12	$60	$720
Domain name	1	$100	$100
Consulting (cybersecurity)	3 mo.	$10,000	$30,000
Software			
Office 365 (licenses and software)	10 users	$12.50/mo.	$1,500
Constant Contact (license per month)	12	$50	$600
CRM (Customer Relations Mgmt)	10 users	$6,000	$6,000
Project mgmt. and other	10 users	$100	$200
Total			$73,520

Resources
Resources listed are suggestions only and should not be regarded as a complete list, endorsements or warranties of any kind.

Accounting software:
For small nonprofits: Sage One (Cloud based), QuickBooks,
For mid-sized nonprofits: QuickBooks Online, Sage 50, Abila MIP Fund Accounting, The Financial Edge

Board Development:
©2017, *Nonprofit Management Simplified: Board and Volunteer Development,* CharityChannel Press, M. L. Donnellan, MS,
www.amazon.com/author/mldonnellan

Budget Templates:
SmartSheets – **https://www.smartsheet.com/free-cost-benefit-analysis-templates**

Cloud Storage:
Dropbox, Box, Google Drive, OneDrive (Microsoft), iCloud

CRM/Donor Management Software:
CiviCRM, Salesforce, SugarCRM, Microsoft Dynamics
https://www.insightly.com
https://www.allclients.com/

Internal Operations Policies and Procedures
©2017, *Nonprofit Management Simplified: Internal Operations,* CharityChannel Press, M. L. Donnellan, MS, **www.amazon.com/author/mldonnellan**

Other helpful software:
FileMaker Pro; FreedCamp, Bitdefender Antivirus, Acrobat Pro; Office 365, HipChat, Tableau Public, Trello, Zoho Expense, StayFocused,

Resource Development
©2017, *Nonprofit Management Simplified: Programs and Fundraising,* CharityChannel Press, M. L. Donnellan, MS,
www.amazon.com/author/mldonnellan

Risk Management and Cybersecurity
"Five Steps to PCI Compliance" -
https://www.alienvault.com/resource-center
https://www.sonicwall.com
PCI security standards:
https://www.pcisecuritystandards.org/
©2017, *Nonprofit Management Simplified: Internal Operations,* CharityChannel Press, by M. L. Donnellan, MS,
www.amazon.com/author/mldonnellan

Strategic Planning
Simplified strategic planning process, ©2017, *Nonprofit Management Simplified: Board and Volunteer Development,* CharityChannel Press, M. L. Donnellan, MS
www.amazon.com/author/mldonnellan

Sustainability
©2016, *Nonprofit Toolkit #2: Sustainability Strategies,* M. L. Donnellan, MS, **www.mldonnellan.com**

Technology grants, equipment and volunteers
TechSoup – **www.techsoup.org**
NetSquared – **www.netsquared.org**
Tech4Good - **https://tech4good.soe.ucsc.edu/#/**
The Foundation Center – **www.foundationcenter.org**
Google Grants - **https://www.google.com/nonprofits/eligibility/**

Volunteer Development
©2017, *Nonprofit Management Simplified: Board and Volunteer Development,* CharityChannel Press, M. L. Donnellan, **www.amazon.com/author/mldonnellan**
©2016, *Nonprofit Toolkit #1: Volunteer Handbook,* M. L. Donnellan, MS, **www.mldonnellan.com**
http://volpro.net/volunteer-management-software-expo/

About the Authors

Marilyn L. Donnellan, MS, has more than 35 years' experience as a nonprofit CEO and consultant. The nonprofits where she served ranged in size from a single staff organization with a budget of $150,000 to a $6 million nonprofit with  300 staff. She is the author of numerous articles in nonprofit trade journals and her books on nonprofit management are in use in more than a dozen countries. She has a B.A. degree in Human Resources Management from George Fox University and an M.S. degree in Administration from Atlantic Coast Theological Seminary.

Margaux S. Pagan has worked in the nonprofit sector for over 15 years, primarily focused on technology-supporting development and fundraising initiatives. Her passion for technology was ignited under the  leadership at the International Fellowship of Christians and Jews. There she led multiple fundraising campaigns and was awarded the Fundraising Star by Fundraising Success Magazine. She has helped nonprofits across the country become tech-centric through her knowledge of website development, database implementations, data analytics, strategic campaign planning and integrated fundraising. Pagan is a graduate of the University of Central Florida.

CPSIA information can be obtained
at www.ICGtesting.com
Printed in the USA
LVOW13s0022040518
575957LV00008B/345/P